this day full of promise

June 22, 2002

Mont St. Odile, France

Gerry,

Keep your stick
on the ice,

your pal,

Michael

this day full of promise: poems selected and new copyright © 2002 Michael Dennis.

Foreword copyright © 2001 rob mclennan.

Cover painting: "Art & Politics" by Dennis Tourbin copyright © 1998. Used by permission of Nadia Laham/the Dennis Tourbin Estate.

Author photo by Kirsty Jackson. Taken in Lytton, BC.

Design and in-house editing by the publisher, Joe Blades.

Printed and bound in Canada by Sentinel Printing, Yarmouth NS.

Simultaneously published, May 2002, as BJP eBook 36, ISBN 1-896647-49-9 (PDF) with distribution via http://PublishingOnline.com.

The publisher acknowledges the support of the Canada Council for the Arts and the New Brunswick Culture and Sport Secretariat-Arts Development Branch.

 cauldron books

A series edited by Ottawa writer/editor/publisher rob mclennan. Named after the Celtic idea of the cauldron as the keeper & dispenser of wisdom & knowledge. The series will focus not only on worthwhile collections of poetry, but on single author collections of essays, as writing on writing. cauldron books are published by Broken Jaw Press. rob may be reached at <az421@freenet.carleton.ca>

Broken Jaw Press
Box 596 Stn A
Fredericton NB E3B 5A6
Canada

www.brokenjaw.com
jblades@nbnet.nb.ca
tel / fax 506 454-5127

National Library of Canada Cataloguing in Publication Data
Dennis, Michael, 1956-
    This day full of promise : poems selected and new / Michael Dennis ; edited with a foreword by Rob McLennan.

(Cauldron books : 2)
Also available in a PDF format.
ISBN 1-896647-48-0

    I. McLennan, Rob, 1970- II. Title. III. Series.

PS8557.E563T44 2002   C811'.54   C2002-901977-X
PR9199.3.D447T44 2002

this day full of promise
poems
selected and new

michael dennis

edited
with a foreword by
rob mclennan

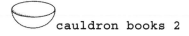 cauldron books 2

Fredericton • Canada

www.boneheadmusic.com/mdennis.htm

for Ann, Jana and Effie, wise women all.

for K.

this day full of promise

foreword

When I first arrived in Ottawa & started looking around, one of the names that stood out on the poetry shelves of used bookstores was michael dennis, from *Fade to Blue*, to the memorably-titled *wayne gretzky in the house of the sleeping beauties*. michael dennis was the first street-level, street-wise poet I discovered in Ottawa, & as I found out, the only one, a generation after the now-legendary William Hawkins, who had done the same, neither one appearing in any of the official anthologies. michael was the first real poet I met in the city.

At his most active, starting his Ottawa days in 1984 to attend Carleton University, dennis was the most published poet in the city, with poems in hundreds of magazines & anthologies across the country. He had started out writing in Peterborough, amid a group of peers that included Maggie Helwig & Richard Harrison, as well as Riley Tench & Dennis Tourbin, who would also end up making the move to Ottawa.

At the height of his activities, the stories are as interesting as the poems, such as the story of the chapbook *how to keep a poet out of jail (or: ship of fools, car of idiots)*, published for friends who had donated money to pay for a driving violation (while intoxicated). As he claims, it's the only book of his he ever made money from. Or the story of *Poems for Jessica-Flynn*, my favourite of his books, written in a month while on display in the window of the long-closed Avenue Bookshop in the Glebe, February 1986. The space at 815½ Bank Street, at Fourth Avenue, is now part of a bakery. (Nine years later, I repeated the project myself, with far less success.) More recently, there is the story of when he read "hockey night in canada" as part of the opening night of the 1999 ottawa international writers festival, & was the crowd favourite, with glowing personal & media reports including in *The Ottawa Citizen* the following morning, overshadowing CanLit icon Pierre Berton.

michael dennis' poems are rough & sexual & sometimes brutally sweet & honest, & have an integrity to them, much as he does. The line between dennis & his poetry is very thin, & follows

7

the working class traditions of Charles Bukowski & Al Purdy, of hard living, & sometimes hard drinking. There are poems about Catherine the Great's sexual appetites, & about Fellini (that makes my skin crawl, still). There are poems about working, & hanging artwork, about Thor, god of fuck, & about michael being in love with his wife.

It was in michael dennis' poems that I first found references to The Royal Oak Pub at Bank & MacLaren Streets, poems that mention drinking pints of toby. When I was twenty years old I took great comfort there, & did the same myself, making the bar my own, for years' worth of writing, knowing that a real writer whose work I admired had done it before me.

rob mclennan
August 2001

...any life expands and flowers only through division and contradiction. What are reason and sobriety without the knowledge of intoxication? What is sensuality without death standing behind it? What is love without the eternal mortal enmity of the sexes?

> Herman Hesse
> *Narcissus and Goldmund*

To remain lucid in ecstasy.

> Bruce Boston
> *Stained Glass Rain*

eastern shore, saltspring island

if these are our creators,
please, please give me something else.

Charles Bukowski

watching the queen on tv

it was shortly after the massacre
we were all glued to the news
children dead in a Scottish town
yet one step closer
to the apocalypse

of course we believed it all
immediately
it is the course of human events
regardless of the extent
of prior villainy
we will make progress
we will do worse

never having been a monarchist
I was surprised
to find myself weeping
at her sadness

it occurred to me
that she was a mother
and seeing the wet red eyes
of other mothers
their homes hysterical
with the silent voices of children
she, the queen,
could no longer maintain
her queenly composure

and it was terribly sad
when she lay the flowers down
you could feel her angst
time and continents away
the unknowable burden
of being the mother of a nation
and the saviour of no one

the sound of a pistol
cracks through the early spring air
a window slams shut
a truck backfires
morning shrugs itself into afternoon
afternoon slides into evening
darkness descends

soft stones

on our backs
sweating in half-laughter
we were holding hands
when the first stone hit

you must realize
the precision necessary
to throw a stone
hard enough
to reach a second storey window
yet softly enough
not to break
the river of glass
flowing between his world and ours

it was clear to me
that he could not see us
but a light was on
and knowing the house
he would know
that is was the small red lamp
at the head of her bed
that she only put on with candles

being my predecessor he would know
that she's put a drop of scented oil
on the pastel red bulb
he would know we could hear him
scuffing his shuffling feet
through the stones in the gutter
making careful decisions
involving weight and mass
distance and velocity
all of this
inside a template of horrible rage

our laughter sucked in air
and she whispered to me
that he wasn't dangerous
the stones lasted another five minutes
we waited ten
between sips of the red
and another smoke

then, the air blue
with hashish and fear
we started in on number three
while the sun began
its inevitable rise
two or three hours to the east

this is a mercy too

born sick and alone
the future is a short, dark moment
nature does this
selects in a fashion
we might consider random

being only men and women
we cannot fathom
a larger plan
our small pains are genuine
we own them
have worked for them
it is through time
that we learn to understand joy
that short
sharp moment

there will always be more hurt
that is the bond we all share
the agreement made as we broach the womb
first comes the light
and then the dark
one utterly incomplete
without the other

when your father leaves you

for Bruce McEwen

it could be an accident
out of nowhere
or the eventual end
of the long sick march
to death
either way
he's gone

you wake up the next morning
and the sun is still shining
the greasy spoon on the corner
has hot coffee, eggs on the grill
you buy the regular, to go

the day is like most others
it runs long in the afternoon
and then the darkness begins
it rolls in from the east
inevitable as everything else

the belly dancer

for Adrian Göllner

you are at a club in Ottawa
lost somewhere in time
Constantinople frames memory

in your movie
a woman is dancing in front of you
her brown skin a test you endure
you can hear her voice
through the red blush of satin
her dark hair splashing sonnets
written to the music of her undulation

when her movement is just so
the scarf wafts slightly skyward
you see the dimple on her chin
it echoes the ruby
that centers your vision

Arabic music laced with lust
the scent of burning cloves
thick liqueur, heavy cigarettes

her voice offers an invitation
it is in a language
you do not recognize

our first night with Count Dracula

for K.

I want to remember
the perfect kiss
where lips meet nirvana
fruit and wine
that moment
where time implodes
black holes illuminate in conflagration
and rainbows dance pretzelled minuets

that kiss
where her hand
holds the back of your neck
with purpose
there is music, of course
but you don't remember it
this kiss renders memory void
wiping out all others
before and until it is bestowed
once more

the high cost of living

for sweet Lou

everything remains the same
on the outside
for now
we are old friends
and mostly I don't notice
the long bathroom sessions
the nodding and the glassy eyes
mostly I don't notice
but I do know

I don't see tracks or needles
but the black smoke rises
and I smell the fear

this kiss too sweet
even for you

this embrace costing
more than any of us
can afford

this day full of promise

let's say you're a deer
and as deer go
you're smarter than average
you're having a good year
whatever it is that you like to eat
is plentiful
you've found an excellent source
of cool, clean water

your summer is going
exactly as you'd planned
your antlers are coming in
things are on target
the doe of your dreams
is doing the doe-eyed thing

it's a Monday morning
although that means nothing
it is just past dawn
you don't know
that your are up wind
from the bear

this is the forest
these are the trees
the flowers are beautiful
and the air is sweet

in the city
madness sometimes descends
in such a random fashion
that if it weren't horror
it would be humour

you could be walking home
from dinner or work
you could be in your bed
under safe sheets

a man approaches
out of the darkness
neither malice nor mayhem
on his mind
he thinks no more evil
than the bear
quiet in the shadows

there is no thought
to the natural order
no safe place
for the hunted

noon shines down directly
as flies skydive
the crimson puddles
the bear
having manifest its will
its destiny
its reason for being
has wandered to a nearby meadow
providence has blown a beehive
from the crooked branches of an aspen
into the sweet toothed path of the bear
there is another
somewhat shaded pool
where dessert and a nap ensue
the bear dreams bear dreams
none better than reality

in the city
the closed windows
of the home
you once lived in
keep in the sound
of blue flies
and the answering machine's
unhappy drone

hours, days, weeks
one of them pass
you're found
but a partner, a friend
the mailman
your story is in the paper

the killer is found
or not
the sun comes up
the following day
with no regrets
and no remorse
this day
as full of promise
as every other
since the beginning of time

my father and I

my father and I are talking on the phone
we've been mostly silent for the last two years

we both have our fears and false memories
we speak different languages about different lives

it is a long reach through 500 miles of wire
but we are making progress and the calls continue

I want some sense of belonging, history
I assume he wants to be forgiven, to be remembered

I think how casually it might have happened
he was at a party and drinking

my mother was there
and she was young and willing

and then I think of the times in my life when all depended
on that moment where she spreads her legs

most of us have been there
longed for that moment, savoured it

morning and consequences
forty years and 500 miles away

Mount St. Helen's reprise

on the evening news
the threat of a new death dance in Africa
the Americans promise to move in
once the killing really starts
(which in some ways
is a new approach for them
and almost humorous
in that "it isn't really our problem" sort of way)

it is the same old fight
someone has what someone wants
and no terms short of violence will do
it could be religion, land or money
it always means power

the banks that run our country
run these countries as well
they are like dinosaurs
the biggest things on the planet
lumbering over the surface
taking what need and avarice demand
not thinking of those volcanoes
all that ash

Charlie Parker
dreams

A poet more than thirty years old is simply
an overgrown child.

H. L. Mencken

he had the knife at her throat

he had the knife at her throat
and I thought we were both
going to die

I was on the floor in the living room
he had knocked me down
with a straight right
and then put the boots to me

I came to, looking at his feet
he was standing over her
with her doggie style on the kitchen floor
he was straddling her back
with the large carving knife
sharp edge up
against the soft underside
of her throat

time stopped
reversed itself
as I cartoon jacked myself
to my feet
as he looked into my eyes
as she screamed
as he raised the blade
towards me
as I ran
as she cried
as he looked at the weapon
in his hands
with both concern and horror
as I jumped
as he dropped the knife
to the counter
and caught me

on the side of my head
with his fist

I woke up
to the sight
of her ankles
being dragged out the door
her scream scratching
at my blurred vision

later
her safety assured
the police gone
an ice bag on my broken nose
I packed my small bag
full of cold beer
and a change of clothes
I got a cab
escaped with my life

on the train
one beer in my left hand for drinking
another in my right
held against my swollen face
to keep my eyes from closing
I remembered those seconds
how time stopped
completely
and I thought
that this is death
this is my end
and was astonished
to find no fear
but only dumb incredulity

the fear came later
as the miles clackity-clacked
beneath me

your favourite table, your favourite bar

you are sitting at your favourite misery table
in the bar you always choose for grief
drinking to watch the mad eyes of possible
dance by the window and horizon
you have been here before
and know exactly what to order

the waitress comes and goes
it is a well-timed sequence
that folds into your monologue of regret
like the cartoon inserts
in the Sunday paper

you think less clearly as each jar empties
knowing the oblivion is by design
the figures in the window become abstract
you realize that you've bonded
with this table, this place, once again
marvel at your ability to sustain
relationships

I dream Charlie Parker dreams

I dream Charlie Parker dreams
when I dream of loving you
where every note of a song
becomes something I can see
the colours slowing down
and light appearing in the spaces
where sound might occur

I see connections I never imagined
a great jazz riff
subtle as a kiss, a whisper
or the smell of you
lingering on the pillows

I hear the bathtub filling
it is a sound coming to me
through sleep and saxophone sighs
an early morning defiance
of the sun and its natural grace

I reach across the expanse
of our marriage bed
to find you
open my eyes
to see you walking towards the bed
naked and smiling
bringing me joy

the morning begins
I jump in

the young boy knows

the young boy knows there is something wrong
knows by the tone of the voices around him
he recognizes the change in emotional temperature
he is too young to know drinking
but he has certainly seen it

he sees some adults disappearing
into mean parodies of themselves
he doesn't know this word
but he senses it all the same
others become sad shadows of themselves
he has had a front row seat
and being mostly silent
he has been left to watch at his leisure

we measure by what we see
experience by accident
we are led by compasses so deeply buried
inside everything we need to hide
we don't see the path
so much as follow our own beacon
hidden somewhere out there in the future
constantly
calling us home

and keep moving forward

we had cycled, that perfect blue morning
to a small fishing village
about twenty kilometres away
as often happens when we ride
a space opened between us
on the road

that space allowed time to consider
time to ponder
time to imagine
to dream
I slowed down
or she sped up
the result the same as always
we met somewhere in the middle
and kept moving forward

we lunched on local wine
an assortment of fresh fish
salad of tomato, cucumber, cheese and olive
a Greek sun off of a postcard

the late afternoon ride home
was mostly downhill and brilliant
our bikes and gravity rocketing us home
to the small apartment we'd rented in Paros

we showered together
and then made love like we were in love
passion without haste

our gentle hour turning to slumber
we woke to a blue horizon
the sun setting yellow
through a white window
a fragrance in the air like cinnamon

the night started somewhere over the steppes of Russia
the sky started to darken over Turkey

we rolled out of our bed
happy as happy could be

the children of strangers

my ex-wife and her husband
have just had their first child
I feel as I should
tremendously happy
for their collective joy

and confused too

in a love
where a child
or the wish for the same
is the battlefield
we find ourselves on
other people's joy
is tempered
with a fine silt jealousy
a gritty guilt
the self-conscious grief
of coveting

we are happy, healthy, strong
yet we hear it sung
but our parents, siblings, friends
we cannot be
truly adult
until we have children
of our own

I see it
in my beautiful wife's eyes
every time she holds a child
how much she loves me
how much I've betrayed

carefully measured

you are hanging pictures
in the waiting room
of a cancer clinic
it is what you do
hanging pictures

there are photos
several of them
forming a series

each of the photographs
is of a greenhouse
there are fields of colour
reflected through
windows of mist
and promise

and with the green
the promise is clear
plants promise life
and this is what
you are thinking

as you carefully measure
distances between nails
checking to make sure
that everything is level

you overhear
hairless conversations
about chemotherapy
and morphine pumps

you mark a spot in pencil
on the wall in front of you
you have to drill a hole
to receive a plug
that will hold a bolt
that will secure the frame
so that nothing will be stolen

your work progresses quickly
as the afternoon
slowly tumbles towards evening
you hear conversations
in brief pieces
one nurse to another
10 cc of this or that
a doctor mentions another test
two patients compare notes

you continue with your work
each part of each second
reminding you
that six years have passed
since your mother died of cancer
since your mother
had these same conversations

everything hung securely
you make sure
to clean the glass
that covers each art work
you collect your tools
and fold them away
to their dark slumber
each in its place
each tool box
properly packed
you push your dolly
loaded with tools

back to your truck
load everything
remembering to tie
each and every object
securely to the metal walls

this, like all other activities
of the day
carefully measured
to ensure safety
passage
success
in this clearly
dangerous world

hockey night in Canada

for Patrik Hunt

early on no one scored
and it stayed like that
for about the first thirty minutes
then a couple of goals snuck in
I got a beauty
there was a mad scramble
in front of the net
and it was one of those ongoing things
someone would blast it in
and the goalie would make the save
and then a defenceman
would pounce on the puck
my goal came off a rebound
I got to it first
the goalie was sprawled
and there was hardly any room
but I was able to get it over him
and put it up on the roof
it was pretty
the game went back and forth
for some time
but then
as time was winding down
I got another break

I took off
and the hounds of hell could not have caught me
Ed Dick flicked a soft pass
out between the two defencemen
and I was off
it was like I had a rocket booster
in my asshole
because I was the god-damned fucking wind

I caught the puck at the red line
and the two big defenders
were right beside me
about five feet apart
but that was all
I felt a stick to each ankle
not a bad stick
or a mean stick
but a "Christ, Michael
slow down!" stick
because you're going to make us look bad
it always looks bad
when the team drunk outskates someone
and this time
I was outskating everyone
lightning wouldn't have caught me
I was speed
I was destiny

I was skating down from center
and in all alone
with every wish
of every boy
who ever laced a skate
I was Howe and Hull
Beliveau and Richard
Paul Henderson against the Russians
I was Bobby Orr
scoring the Stanley Cup winner
against the St. Louis Blues
I was George Armstrong
the old Chief
hitting that empty net
the last time the Leafs won in '67
I was Gretzky and Lemieux
skating down on that poor red son of a bitch
with destiny throwing me a glad hand

and a ticket to Siberia
for that borscht-eating bastard
I hit the blueline
like a freight train
hitting a fruit wagon
I hit the blueline like
Mario "I'll drive any fucking thing on this planet faster that
you" Andretti
hitting the gas hard
I hit the blueline
like a snake
called for the strike
you never see
I hit the blueline
at the speed of sound
and was gaining
on the speed of light

I heard every cheer
of every fan
from every game
from the beginning of time
to eternity
and they were all on their feet
and rocking
and I may never have been good before
and I may never be good again
but I was great
I was flying
I was soaring
I was a bird
in perfect and natural grace
sweeping out and down from the heavens
whistling Beethoven's fifth out of my asshole
while painting the *Mona Lisa* with my toes
I was on my back
and doing what Michelangelo did in the chapel

I was great Caesar's ghost and then some
I was grace and beauty
and the goalie didn't have a chance

he had no more chance
than the blonde in the opening of *Jaws*
no more chance
than a drink
in a thirsty man's hand
I came down on him
like the charge of the Light Brigade
down on him like a herd of buffalo
before the white man came
and pissed it all away
I came down on him
and made a move to my backhand
that left him and his equipment
wishing they were in another place
wishing they were anywhere other than here
wishing he had someplace to hide
because this god-damned short
fucking drunk bastard
is going to kill me
he is my murderer
and my assassin
and my end and my destiny
and he is not going to leave me
anything but the memory
of the net I once protected
he is going to disgrace me
and every save I ever made
all of it wiped out
in one move
that was so pure
and so perfect
so made for this moment
that the goalie might as well

have not been there
because this was written
before we put on our skates
before we were born
it was written
when the fish crawled out of the sea
and asked for directions
it was written
when those hairy French cavemen
first put something on a wall

I faked to my left
to my backhand
and for all I know
the goalie is still wondering
where I went
because I went by him
like a thought
I went by him
like he didn't exist
and then I put that fucker in the corner
as sweet as Ali let Foreman
know what destiny is all about
a little kiss to the back of the net
as sweet as Dr. J.
dunkin' it with his glorious, glorious beauty

I was still travelling
at the speed of two lovers
I was still going fast enough
to go through the end boards
standing up
but that couldn't happen
it would all be for naught
if the ending was as perfect
as the rest
I turned on a dime

as I grazed the boards
I was on rails
I was a slot car
a train
I was everything
you always dreamed it could be

in the dressing room
guys from both teams congratulated me
each sharing in what they knew
was unlikely to happen again
and each just a little pleased
for having been part of it
the goalie mentioned
that he remembered the goal
from the scramble
but not the breakaway
and I am not surprised

if I thought I was dreaming
maybe we all were
maybe it didn't happen
maybe the roar I heard
was just blood pounding
in my Southern Comfort cured brain
but I don't think so
I felt it
it was pure
and real
and it happened
just like I said
every word
as true as it gets

the ongoing dilemma of small change

how the real romantic thinks

flowers
there must always be flowers
buy her flowers when you love her
but more importantly
buy her flowers when you don't
wine is essential
always remember the wine
red wine in the winter
red wine in the fall
spring and summer demand white
try spanish or italian
but do not forget the flowers

marvel at her beauty
and insist knowingly
that her wardrobe is like jewellery
beautiful, but only an accent
to her natural charms

open doors for her
always
hold her chair at dinner
do not assume she needs these things
but rather
that they are gifts
and the pleasure is in the giving

it is not the kiss
but the idea

I share an apartment with two artists

so I went to go to the bathroom
it had been a long night
too many beer
the morning sun was screaming in the window
that it was time to piss
I am the obedient sort
I raced down the hall to the bathroom
to find the window covered with a black sheet
the bathtub full of chemicals
and a developer sitting on the toilet
I was desperate
and the sink was handy

I was also in need of a bath
I emptied the tub
washed down the yogurt and sulphur smell of the chemicals
and filled the tub with the hot water that would save me

as usual, I sank to my chin
got the paper wet while I read the news
the steam of the tub soothed
while the odour of chemicals
swirled thoughtlessly through the room

when I got out to dry myself off
my skin was its usual post-bath lobster red
I sprinkled myself liberally with baby powder
and got dressed to face the day

as I walked down the stairs
and towards the street
I could feel pictures
beginning to develop
on my chest and thighs

go to sleep

go to sleep

suppose you were one of Charlie Manson's parents
and everyone knew it
you go to buy groceries
and everyone stares at you
you get anonymous letters asking
"when's Charlie coming home?
 Have we got a surprise for him"

maybe you tell everyone that you aren't really related
but then the mailman tells them
that Charlie writes every day
the letters have s.w.a.k. in a scrawl
on the backs of the envelopes

when you sleep
you have dreams on a split screen
on one half
young Charlie, wearing blue shorts
and bringing home his first report card
it could even be straight As

the other half of the dream
you are running out of the house
Charlie is chasing you
he has blood on his fingers
and a knife in his teeth

so being one of Charlie's parents
sometimes you get letters from the parents
of the children that moved in with Charlie
they ask how and why
but not really specific questions
just the vague longing of incomprehension

no matter where you go
you think that people are staring
and you know that you've done nothing wrong
but you can hear whispers
always whispers

it's okay
you can wake up now
Charlie was an orphan
or close to it
he did what he had to
what he was always going to
just like you

dancing with Miss Kitty

watching reruns of *Gunsmoke*
I've begun to suspect
that Miss Kitty
is not only poking Doc
but poking Festus too
Matt being as naive as he is
simply isn't catching on
but Miss Kitty is getting it
from Doc for intellectual stimulation
and Festus because he's hung like a mule

she must be
there are no other women in Dodge
and we all know what red hair means

every Sunday morning I turn on the set
Matt is out of town
while Miss Kitty is having breakfast
with Doc or Festus or both
which brings to mind the image
of the three of them
drunk and thrashing about
in one of Miss Kitty's rooms
Festus with his socks and hat on
and Miss Kitty in nothing but a grin
it is the only time Doc and Festus don't argue

of course Matt protects Miss Kitty's virtue
and Festus and Doc protect Matt
the circle of innocence remains unbroken
Sunday morning
exactly as it should be

campbell's cream of piano soup

for Tom Robbins and Thelonious Monk

"call the Doctor on the phone..."
NRBQ

she answered all his questions with music
he asked her how her day had been
and she played Louis Armstrong
on the stereo
the rasp of his voice
asking for kisses
to build dreams on

he asked her for a kiss
and she played coltrane
and dolphy
whistling wild whispers
about favourite things

he asked her if she would stay
and she put on monk
turned the volume up
and put out the lights

the next day
when he woke
there was a copy of her heart
tattooed to her pillow
kisses on the mirror in the hall

she was nowhere to be seen

when he went into the living room
he saw her shadow spinning
it was on the turntable
going round and round and round

Catherine's horse, don't you know

did you know that Catherine the Great died
because of a horse
true story

you see
Catherine had what you might call
a desire to explore
she had numerous maidens working for her
they were to sleep with members of the guard
and select those best equipped
to attend to Catherine's desire

so what happened was this
she had a special machine commissioned
and the machine broke

what was supposed to happen
was that the machine would lower a horse
down on top of the willing Catherine

I'm far too shy to go into the details
of what the horse was supposed to do
let's just say they her need was equestrian

when they tried lowering the horse
the machine broke
the horse's considerable weight came crashing down

now this raises numerous questions
such as
was this the first time
she tried using the machine
did it break as soon as they tried it
or did Catherine, that sly fox
get a few hours
and a few giggles first

now of course you realize
that this is all in the interest of truth
the passing on of our history

why, I once heard that Napoleon
sent his wife a letter from the front
and it ended with
Josephine, my darling
I'll be home in two weeks
don't bathe

you and your dog Toto too

you are sitting on your balcony
drinking your evening beer
you see a blur pass before your eyes
the blur is the exact size of a small dog
the exact size of a small dog
falling at the speed
a dog would fall
if thrown from an eleventh floor window

you are unsure of what you've seen
but you have the beer
and the evening is just beginning

minutes later
there is another blur
it is bigger and more vocal
you think you may even recognize
the woman who is falling
you have seen her before

what happened is:
a married couple fighting
they have a dog
she likes and he doesn't
they are drinking
the dog shits on the floor
and in a drunken rage
he throws it out the window
she replies with teeth bared
red-tipped fingers slashing
so
he throws her out the window too

as she is falling past your balcony
you hear her screaming
and recognize her from the elevator
she is the woman who always has
the dog in her arms
she always has the dog in her arms
and talks to it like a lover

fish in the ocean, tears in the sea

we have moved to the ocean
and spend as much time at the beach
as we can possibly manage
all the myths mean nothing
but the ocean truly soothes
the endless waves massage the heart
and the soul
and that is what we need

so hopelessly in love with each other
we are unable to guard
from the arrows of our desire
our passion sometimes finding direction
in paths that lead away from our home
lead to beds that do not recognize
our marriage

and there is no blame to be considered
no fingers to point
only the days
one stacked on another
each one our past
the promise of each
our future

we weather the storms
of emotional hurricane and tidal wave
rest easy when the ocean is calm
we are not deceived by blue sky and gentle sea
but rather
enjoy the good sail
while we can
batten down the hatches
when the sky threatens black

birthmarks

I used to tell girls my real name was Thor
Thor, God of fuck
I have the birthmark to prove it
it's on my rear end
I can't remember which side
but I have a small brown birthmark
that is shaped like a lightning bolt

I imagine myself in the heavens
sharing my godly flesh
with a willing goddess
her thrashing into me
with unequalled passion
the sounds of our lovemaking
rolling like thunder over the earth
crashing with sparks and flame
our coming together
an earthquake and tidal wave
that leaves no survivors

but then there is the other side
my mother used to tell me
that because I was such a brat
my birthmark was a shit stain
that just wouldn't come out
she told me
that I used to torment her
by reaching into my soiled diapers
and painting the walls
with my discovery
she swears I was not born with the mark
but rather it grew on me
increasing in size
as her torment grew more ferocious

a birthmark
of another kind

spring

for Louis Patrick Fagan and Connor Charles St.Michael

the promise of flowers haunts our future memory
as the true calendar of weather begins to reveal the earth
winter, for all its mirthful snow is a mean bastard of a thing
and we are thankful to see it go

spring is so much more than promise
all things begin, we move forward
out of the cold coma of hibernation
and into the frenzy of a mystic sun
the reborn earth psychedelic with colour and glee
spring is a joyous shout to the gods of immortality
a saintly whisper that allows us to sing
that we are still here and full of hope
that we will continue to love
to bathe in the blue sky green earth splendour
that we choose the flower and the fruit once more
that we cannot and will not forget
the harsh lessons of another winter

but we feel this in our bones
this giant human need to celebrate life
to grow new crops, paint new pictures
to fall in love - mad glorious love
with everyone and everything

that these sentiments are not new is no burden
we are as we have always been
women and men, boys and girls
a living part of a living world
getting another chance
delighted once again

the ongoing dilemma of small change

we were sitting in a Greek restaurant
and remembering our time in Greece
our table was in the window
with the sun coming in hard
catching us full on the face
the illusion was easy
blue sky, white sand

until a drunken man
collapsed into the window
gravity and glass conspiring against him

he quickly righted himself
and navigated a slow arcing shuffle
down the street
towards miserable sobriety
or the glow of more wine

I know people who refuse to give change
if they figure it will go to drink

I find that life sometimes weighs heavy
after a long day of work
and when it does
I love a glass of red to soothe the beast

I find that life is frequently joyous
I'm healthy
in love and fully loved
unable to dance appropriately
I sometimes celebrate
with a glass of white
the cold music of grace
hypnotizing
as it soars and blesses

life is hard enough
for all of us

we were lovers and i think friends

i was teaching english
at a factory in czechoslovakia
and she was one of my students
in class she wore her work dress
and grease covered wooden clogs
the first time she came to my home
she had on a white silk shirt
and black leather pants
we became lovers
and it was glorious
until her beast of an ex-husband
broke into my apartment
and beat us both into a new reality
my czech was poor
but it was good enough to know
that he intended to kill me
given a second chance
the czech police were useless
and the canadian embassy hogtied
i left pardubice that night
with a knapsack of ice-cold beer
i held one to my swelling face
as i sat in a berth full of soldiers
young men returning to praha
to serve their country
jitka and i talked on the phone
and met in other towns
but it was hopeless
she couldn't leave pardubice
and i couldn't stay

we were lovers and i think friends
tell me if she still walks the factory floor
if her mother and son misha are ok
we were lovers and i think friends
and i miss her part of the world

Belgium, England, Scotland

again, for Gary

Primus Haacht, Stella Artois,
Maes Pils, Jupiler, Bass Pale Ale,
Duvel, Tetley Bitter, Burtonwood Bitter,
Castlemaine XXXX, Breaker Strong Lager,
Younger's Kestrel Pilsner Lager,
Worthington Best Bitter, Bass Special Bitter,
Harp Lager, Webster's Yorkshire Bitter,
John Smith's Bitter, Titan Lager,
Theakston Best Bitter, Stone's Best Bitter,
McEwan's Lager, McEwan's 80/-Heavy,
Bellhaven Best, Tennent's Charger Lager,
McEwan's Export Strength, Burton's Real Ale,
Caledonian 80/-, Deuchar's IPA, Tetley
Traditional Ale, St. Andrew's Ale, Boddinton
Bitter, Pedigree Bitter

Parikia, Greece

why i don't like fellini

imagine a twenty-year-old woman
she is lying on the beach
getting a tan
perhaps her back is getting a little too much sun
there are pink lines where the straps of her top usually cross
she is laying on her stomach
the sand is warm and feels good
she is daydreaming
in her mind her arms are around a young man
they are kissing

she feels a sting on her left cheek
just below her eye
without thinking
reflex brings her hand to her face
and she removes a small black and red spider
she shudders and quickly leaves the beach
hastily tying her bathing suit
and feeling at her cheek with a testing hand

later that night her cheek is red and slightly swollen
she promises herself she will see the doctor in the morning
but when she wakes it is gone
there is no pain and no swelling
by afternoon she is in the bar with friends
and has forgotten the entire thing

two months later
while dressing in front of the mirror
she notices a small swelling under her left eye
by midday it is a noticeable lump
and by the following morning
it is a fairly large growth
she touches it constantly and although there is no pain
her fingers return to it again and again
(the tongue always returns to the cavity, plays with the pain)

while she is touching it
it explodes like a boil
instead of spewing forth the expected puss and blood
dozens of small black spiders literally fly out of her face
she is shocked and then screaming
the spiders continue to empty themselves from her cheek
free after an abnormal gestation

several months later
the same once beautiful young woman is still in the hospital
she cannot look in the mirror
cannot bring herself to touch her own flesh
she becomes hysterical at the sight of spiders

the night hangs its heroes
leaving the morning to bury its dead

the horn growled
against the darkness
he beat against it
till his hands bled
his headlights aimed
at her window
neighbours calling the police
and no one coming to the door
the young man
mad with love
and lust
and desire
and hate
and revenge
and sympathy
and hope
and forever
and her eyes
and his dreams
and the future
and promises
and summer nights
and sincerity
and pain
and blood
and flowers
and her smell
and poetry
and the silence of the nighttime
and the laughter of the dawn
and her kiss
and rage
and forever
and forever
and forever

because you're fucked up and I'm perfectly sane

I don't have to listen to you
I can cross the light
on the colour of my choice
I can wear mismatched socks
I can listen to Mozart one minute
and Monk the next
I can make love any time of the day or night
I can watch movies all day Wednesday
and not feel guilty
I can drink Coca-Cola at breakfast
I can run backwards like a dog
I can walk on my hands
without emptying my pockets
I can wear a ponytail to the Red Cross
I can read Proust and Popeye in the same night
I can fly when given half the chance

when the band calls for tender dancing

even though she has just come
you don't let go
you have your arms wrapped around
so that your hands are on her ass
one of her cheeks
in each of your palms
your mouth is buried
so that your tongue is inside her
she does not object
but instead
is still rocking slowly
from her last orgasm

when you start on her again
there is no time in this dimension
not much of anything
beyond where mouth meets clit
with eyes closed there is no other world
nothing but this hunger
this passion
this feast

on the death of bob kaufman

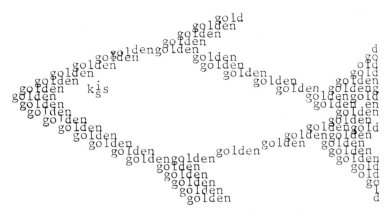

sardines

how the poet thinks

so now I'm really doing it
I mean really looking like a poet
you know how it is
I have the sunglasses on
and am sitting in the window
hammering away at the typer
with a bottle of red opened
and at my feet
pretty girls walk by
and most of them smile
when they do anything at all
the cars take no notice
and I don't particularly care
the sun is beating down
and cooking things in here
but it doesn't matter
I'm wearing my beer-stained workpants
I've got the typer straddled
like a whore might have a lover
and I'm beating into it
hammering away
not making sense of the thing
but just pounding
to make sure I'm alive

Wayne Gretzky in the house of the sleeping beauties

I am watching hockey on television
after all, I am a Canadian boy
but I am also reading, I am a poet as well
it is a novelette by the Japanese writer Kawabata
the story of a man who frequents a bordello of sorts
but it is a bordello for old men only
men who are no longer able to have sex
they go to this house and sleep beside beautiful young women
who have been drugged and are naked and oh so beautiful
I am reading this, my eyes full of Japanese women
and lotus blossoms and then of course
that God damned Gretzky scores, it is inevitable
he is always scoring - but I do not mind
I think of Gretzky as an artist
and feel honoured to watch him work
I do not imagine him writing delicate Japanese prose
or taking Cecil Beaton type photographs
like those in the book I'm holding on my lap
to use as a desk while I write this
but I am a Canadian boy and the artistry
of sticks and skates is something I understand

tonight I dream many dreams
winter and skating on a rink that never ends
in another dream I am wearing a kimono
my eyes are closed and my lips waiting
in this dream I am thinking nipples
and the endless variety, beauty
I imagine that I am with all the girls
in Kawabata's House of the Sleeping Beauties
it is wonderful

and where does this all end
some incomprehensible metaphor
about hockey and Japanese women
the slash of skates into ice
like a knife into flesh
a strange version of Hari-Kairi
and I think no, none of these things
I watch Gretzky
score another goal

somewhere over another rainbow

somewhere over the rainbow
when i'm especially high
there's a place i like to remember
a forgotten lullaby

sing this to the old tune
and think of judy garland
sitting like a sparrow
in that bathroom that meant death

it has come to this
being old enough
to feel nostalgia

no longer understanding the music
not being able to keep in time
my awkward attempts at rhythm
the spastic convulsions
of someone desperate
to cling to the only raft in sight
while beneath and around him
the sharks circle
shark smiles on their faces
white teeth gleaming

the future

this is life
what can we do
at the hospital
in a quiet moment
I go into the hall
for any noise
any sign of life

an old woman
in a wheelchair
rolls by in a pathetic
one foot push
I offer her assistance
and hear
a psychotic ramble
the woman is sad
alone and lonely
but she is alive

my sleeping friend
is headed
in the other direction

I walk to the end of the hall
and hear all those old voices
I was here
when my mother died
when the Twister left too
it is all the same old story
this is life
what can we do

I go back
to my friend
the silence piercing all sound
like some far off sunburst
that crashes through time

the rings around
the sound of the light
breaking over us
like a timeless wave
of rain

at the hospital
nurses appear on the horizon
back and forth
like hope
like promise

but they are human
and can change nothing
the future rushes in
like
the tired old horse
it is

working again

it's been six years or more
but I'm back
at the museum
walking those long curved halls
taking in all that history
all that dust

it's great to be working
after the last six months
of sitting
on my can
and waiting

for a job
for a break
for a kick in the ass

I took my wife
out to dinner
on Friday night
we went Japanese

for the first time
in months
when the bill came
I kept it
pulled out my clip
and pulled off seven twenties

gave the waitress a nod
took my wife by the hand
and stepped outside
into the illuminated night

it had been
a long time
since I'd felt
like a winner
she held my hand
like she always does
but I felt
just that much taller
riding a bit of luck

dreaming about suicide

a man named george
who was something like an uncle
set fire to his farm
and then backed his car into a snowbank
full of carbon monoxide dreams
his life reduced
to some awkward puzzle
of lunacy and sorrow
by the complications
of being a poor dirt-farmer
and the tragedies a family endures

another distant relative
beheaded himself
the day he retired
he was so despondent
about his future
that he jammed a chainsaw
between a rock and a hard spot
and the gravity of flesh prevailed

i am sitting across from a church
watching the world through a window
thinking that if either of them
were to have asked me
i would have no answers
for any of their questions
not condoning their deaths
but understanding

saw my second psychiatrist today
and i'm feeling much better about the world

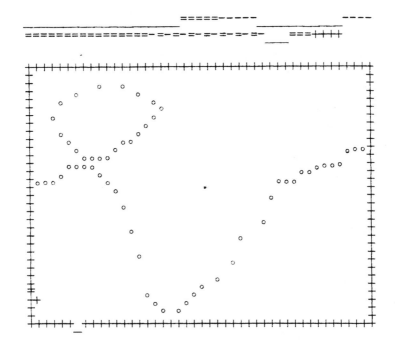

Mayakovsky

tortured with love
he put gun to chest
and blew a hole
where his heart should be

in his note
to the living
he left these words
for his lover

"love me"

what else
could possibly be said

poem for Jessica-Flynn

the name Jessica-Flynn
came to me in a dream
it was to be the name
of our first born child
when I was living
with an actress of subtle
and magnificent beauty

when we finally broke up
it was not a question of love
our dreams no longer mattered
in the confusion and anger
that barely concealed our fear

the scariest part of the entire affair
was the knowing
that love hadn't failed
that we still felt deeply and sincerely
about each other
but that it wasn't enough
and that there was no way to share
what we had thought
would be an ideal life

there was no hope of ever having a child together
and with that loss no hope of ever having children
it would become a gamble too great to chance
a gamble I would never be brave enough to take

when we separated Jessica-Flynn died
as surely
as if she had been torn
from the womb

other publications by Michael Dennis

quarter on its edge
just standin' in the rain, talkin' to myself
poems for one-eyed jacks
sometimes passion, sometimes pain
no saviour and no special grace
poems for jessica-flynn
christmas on the nile
so you think you might be judas
how to keep a poet out of jail (or: ship of fools, car of idiots)
wayne gretzky in the house of the sleeping beauties
portrait
fade to blue
what we remember and what we forget
missing the kisses of eloquence
the ongoing dilemma of small change
what we pass over in silence
no gravy, no garlands, no bright lights

A Selection of Our Titles in Print

A Fredericton Alphabet (John Leroux) photos, architecture	1-896647-77-4	14.95
Avoidance Tactics (Sky Gilbert) drama	1-896647-50-2	15.88
Bathory (Moynan King) drama	1-896647-36-7	14.95
Break the Silence (Denise DeMoura) poetry	1-896647-87-1	13.95
Combustible Light (Matt Santateresa) poetry	0-921411-97-9	12.95
Crossroads Cant (Mary Elizabeth Grace, Mark Seabrook, Shafiq, Ann Shin.		
Joe Blades, editor) poetry	0-921411-48-0	13.95
Cuerpo amado/Beloved Body (Nela Rio; Hugh Hazelton, translator)		
poetry	1-896647-81-2	15.88
Dark Seasons (Georg Trakl; Robin Skelton, trans.) poetry	0-921411-22-7	10.95
Day of the Dog-tooth Violets (Christina Kilbourne) novel	1-896647-44-8	17.76
for a cappuccino on Bloor (kath macLean) poetry	0-921411-74-X	13.95
Great Lakes logia (Joe Blades, ed.) art & writing anthology	1-896647-70-7	16.82
Heart-Beat of Healing (Denise DeMoura) poetry	0-921411-24-3	4.95
Heaven of Small Moments (Allan Cooper) poetry	0-921411-79-0	12.95
Herbarium of Souls (Vladimir Tasic) short fiction	0-921411-72-3	14.95
I Hope It Don't Rain Tonight (Phillip Igloliorti) poetry	0-921411-57-X	11.95
Jive Talk: George Fetherling in Interviews and Documents (George Fetherling;		
editor Joe Blades)	1-896647-54-5	13.95
Manitoba highway map (rob mclennan) poetry	0-921411-89-8	13.95
Notes on drowning (rob mclennan) poetry	0-921411-75-8	13.95
Peppermint Night (Vanna Tessier) poetry	1-896647-83-9	13.95
Railway Station (karl wendt) poetry	0-921411-82-0	11.95
Reader Be Thou Also Ready (Robert James) novel	1-896647-26-X	18.69
Rum River (Raymond Fraser) fiction	0-921411-61-8	16.95
Shadowy Technicians: New Ottawa Poets (ed. rob mclennan)		
poetry	0-921411-71-5	16.95
Singapore (John Palmer) drama	1-896647-85-5	15.88
Song of the Vulgar Starling (Eric Miller) poetry	0-921411-93-6	14.95
Speaking Through Jagged Rock (Connie Fife) poetry	0-921411-99-5	12.95
Starting from Promise (Lorne Dufour) poetry	1-896647-52-9	13.95
Tales for an Urban Sky (Alice Major) poetry	1-896647-11-1	13.95
The Longest Winter (Julie Doiron, Ian Roy) photos, fiction	0-921411-95-2	18.69
These Are My Elders (Chad Norman; Heather Spears, ill.)	1-896647-74-X	13.95
The Sweet Smell of Mother's Milk-Wet Bodice		
(Uma Parameswaran) fiction	1-896647-72-3	13.95
This Day Full of Promise: Poems Selected and New		
(Michael Dennis, rob mclennan (editor) poetry	1-896647-48-0	15.88
Túnel de proa verde/Tunnel of the Green Prow (Nela Rio;		
Hugh Hazelton, translator) poetry	0-921411-80-4	13.95
What Was Always Hers (Uma Parameswaran) fiction	1-896647-12-X	17.95

www.brokenjaw.com hosts our current catalogue, submissions guidelines, manuscript award competitions, booktrade sales representation and distribution information. Directly from us, all individual orders must be prepaid. All Canadian orders must add 7% GST/HST (Canada Customs and Revenue Agency Number: 12489 7943 RT0001). Broken Jaw Press eBooks (in PDF format) of selected titles are available from http://www.PublishingOnline.com.
BROKEN JAW PRESS, Box 596 Stn A, Fredericton NB E3B 5A6, Canada